4 REIGNER
2 REALITY

Aria Page Tucker &
Bryan Craig Tucker

Table of Contents

12 step poem 7

#1 13

#2 16

#3 18

#4 19

#5 20

#6 22

#7 23

#8 25

#9 27

#10 28

#11 29

#12 30

#13 31

#14 32

#15 33

#16 35

#17 36

#18 37

#19 38

#20 39

#21 40

#22 41

#23 42

#24 44

#25 45

#26 46

#27 47

#28 49

#29 50

#30 51

#31 52

#32 53

#33 54

#34 55

#36 56

#37 58

#38 59

#39 60

#40 61

#41 62

#42 64

#43 66

#44 67

#45 68

#46 69

#47 70

#48 71

#49 73

#50 74

The Good Ol' Days

Remember the years when we enjoyed launching hot balls of firey lead into the distant mounds of dirt without ever asking questions first? Can you recall that the answer to life at that time was so straightforward and simple? The solution was to violently inhale more of that sweet, addicting aroma known as carbon which was produced by the discharging propellant. A young infantryman simply bathing in his own truth while the uncertainty of the future was served up constantly for breakfast, lunch, dinner, and dessert. Upon arrival at basic training, everything was sheer insanity and abnormal. As the hours, days, weeks, and years flowed by a Soldier, the insanity quickly and deeply became engrained as completely sane and normal. The unnaturals one day become natural, like the act of breathing and exhaling. The brain now has this internal voice wired to go to war against some external enemy, a common yet invisible enemy. Imagine you went ghost or monster hunting and came out with the realization that you may be the ghost or monster. Trained, prepared, and played hide and seek for and with this beast over the years. A knuckle-dragging fool who rucked every which direction down many paths up many mountains. One day, everyone starts intensely gazing out at the mirrored abyss and notices that the reflection is staring back. It's patiently waiting on your next poker move. You only have the option to Call, bluff, fold, or raise, and your shadow will simultaneously match your every move. Face to face now with the past, present, and future, the mirror will tell the truth as it reflects the entity projected within as same and such. There is no escaping the mirror of the mind. It is a prison that we tend to confine ourselves to unconsciously or consciously, and it transforms into our own heavenly hell or hellacious heaven. The high felt when the noise echoes from the fins of mortar shells banging off the rim of a tube. An irreplaceable rush felt from dropping down a tube and sending an ordinance of doom miles away and hearing the reverberation of the explosion travels back through space and time itself. If that wasn't enough adrenaline, then perhaps the screams of a 240-machine gun ripping apart the silence of the night was. Endless 7.62mm fire awakening, all within range, which was always soon joined by waves of 5.56mm support. The whole goal was to embed, implant, and force the "Devil" himself into the dirt with zero opportunity or desire to stand up. The prince of darkness would mercifully fear for life and beg God to end the lead shower. It wasn't a matter of whether one actually got the opportunity to meet this "evil" energy properly or if one was never presented with the chance to introduce himself. The circus must continue to travel on, and the real freaks loved spending and expending all ammunition regardless of budgets. This carnival of degenerates grew confidence within the self and everyone else. The crew always started with an excellent leader. An exceptional leader who would entrust, empower, inspire, and pressure the other members of the platoon to evolve into their own forces that are one day a force to be reckoned with. A true leader, to me at least, is one consisting of an amalgamation of many different philosophies, the capability to be different animals while remaining the same beast, and the empathy to differentiate between similarities and disparities.

12 step poem

Step One

Admit The Truth

Life Has Lost Its Gentle Youth

Powerless Consumed By Fear

The Path Ahead Wasn't Clear

Step Two

Believe In Love Divine

A Higher Power

A Sacred Sign

A Beacon Shining In The Night

Guiding Towards The Path Of Light

Step Three

Surrender Let It Go

Release The Burdens Let Them Flow

Within The Hands Of The Divine

A New Beginning Will Align

Step Four

Reflect Look Within

Unravel The Layers Of All Your Sin

Embrace The Past The Pain The Sorrow

For Healing Begins With A New Tomorrow

Step Five

Confess Speak The Truth

To Another Soul

A Sacred Booth

Release The Secrets

Let Them Go

Find Freedom In The Truth You Show

Step Six

Accept

Embrace Change

Defy The Urges To Rearrange

Let Humility Guide Your Way

As You Navigate Each Passing Day

Step Seven

Humbly Ask For Grace

In Times Of Struggle

Seek A Place

Where Forgiveness Reigns Supreme

And Mercy Flows Like A Gentle Stream

Step Eight

Make Amends

Seek Peace

With Those You've Hurt

Let Conflicts Cease

Make Right The Wrongs Of Yesterday
And Pave The Path For A Brighter Way

Step Nine

Reach Out

Make Things Right

Amend The Past

With All Your Might

Apologize

Heal The Pain

And Let Forgiveness Gently Reign

Step Ten

Reflect

Each Day Anew

Stay Vigilant

Keep Thoughts Simple And True

Continue On The Path You've Set

With Grace And Gratitude

Yet Never Forget

Step Eleven

Seek Serenity

In Moments Of Quiet

Find Clarity

Connect With The Divine Above

And Feel The Presence Of Endless Love

Step Twelve

Carry The Message Now

Of Hope And Courage

Show Them How

Guide Others On The Path You've Marched

And Share The Gift Of A Higher God As You Walk

Dr. Jekyll & Mr. Hyde

In That Bag & Bottle

Evil Spirits Hide

Their Essence Is Trapped, Waiting Inside

When The Top Pops & A Bag Is Stocked

Wickedness Is Certainly Unlocked

The Sorcerer's Powers Start To Abide

In Shadows Deep

Where Spirits Roam

A Soul In Light

No Longer Alone

12 Steps To Freedom

12 Steps To Grace

In The Fellowship

Of A Sacred Place

In Shadows Deep

Where Demons Dance

Where Minds Grow Foggy

Hearts In Trance

In Halls Of Vice

Where Temptation Lurks

A Weary Soul

Alone To Work

The Poison Drips

The Bottle Calls

A Siren Song

That Slowly Mauls

The Will To Fight

The Will To Be

Beneath The Spell

Comes Death's Calvary

The Needle Pricks

The Pills Dissolve

The Spirits Rise

The Fears Absolve

But In The End

What Did They Gain?

A Hollow High

A Burning Pain

Through Hazy Nights

And Blurry Days

The Addiction's Grip

Relentlessly Stays

A Cycle Spun Of Pleasure

And Woe

A Never-Ending

Ebb And Flow

#1

A Difference

I Have Traveled Far
To Study The Story Of Man
Past Stations Of Knowledge
Past's Creed And Clan
Past Sorrow And Mourning
Nights Full Of Pain & Hate
I Have Traveled Far
And Arrived Too Late
Now, I Am Told
Advised Every Day
My Study Is Wasted
For Here Is What Some Say

"Man Is An Equal
Whether He Is Wise
For The Book Is Useless
To His Open Eyes

The Man In The Street
Who Never Saw A School
Learned As A Scholar
But The Scholar Is A Fool

Such Is The Story
I Hear Every Day
I Think About The Energy
I Have Wasted Away

Twenty Years With The Classics
Twelve On The Road
Oh In Memory
I Carry Such Load

The Standards And Fashions
The Ethics I'll Say
The Rudiments Of Music
And The Signs At Play

The Total Of Life
The Magical Call
I've Wasted These Years
Studying Them All?

I've Wasted These Years
So Say, My Friends
Still, Nothing Is Wasted
Till A Poor Life Ends

Over And Over, I Still Think
Many Of Years That I Have Drank
What Is Meant For The Eye

And Comes By Surprise

Maybe Silence Is The Greatest Reply

So It Is From Knowledge Of Creed & Clan

I Am Able To Swear

There's A Difference In The Man

#2

"Wild Geese Flying" *Author's Actual Experience*

I Watched Your Flight
Out Of Pattern Against An Evening Sky
Barely Discernible
I Followed You By Your Loud And Plaintive Cry

I Saw You In Confused Disorder
Scanning The Earth Below
Waiting For Your Trusted Courser
To Point The Way To Go

Weary You Seemed And Uncertain
I Guessed It By Your Cry
Gone Was Your Graceful Precision
You Seemed As Lost As I

I Thought Of The Miles Before You
And Wondered If You Could Surmise
That A Kindred Soul Below You
Watched With Anxious Eyes

Soon Your Flight Took Pattern
Like An Arrow Pointing True
And Gathering Speed In Moments
You Soon Were Lost To View

And As I Sat Lost In Reverie

I Found My Own Fears Had Fled

And That My Soul Had Taken Wings

And I Followed Where You Led

#3

Serenity

Shall We Accept

Karma That The Universe Sends Our Way

Lord Knows We Can Accept The Things

That We Cannot Change

God Grants Wisdom To Understand The Difference & Same

Can You Hear The Thunder?

Now, Who Stops The Rain?

#4

Lotus 4 You, A Buddha 2 Be
Is It 54 Or 42?
Seek More
If You Haven't A Clue
What Is A Lie
In A World Full Of Truths?
Strange Phenomena & Mysterious Ways
Types Of Events
Creating Order From Disarray
In A World Of Tangled Tales & Doubts
The Truth Is Genuinely There
Yet, It Subtly Shrouds
You Seek The Proof & Evidence
That No One Can Find
To Quench Your Skepticism
With Divine Logic Aligned
A Lotus 4 You, A Buddha 2 Be
Enjoy The High Beyond Ecstasy

#5

OH MY GOD!

I Met YOU Twice Today

Two Past Sinners, Now They Are Saints?

Those Kind You Occasionally Meet Who Selflessly Go Far Out Of Their Own Way

They Simply Helped A Man Who Doesn't Know How To Process His Thoughts On What To Say

What If One Man Actually Did Meet All 8 Billion People On Earth?

Would They All Be Different But Strangely The Same?

God, I Use To Think It Was The World That Had Gone Insane

Then I Looked In The Mirror Today And Must Shoulder All That Blame

Listening To Your Voice As Your Words Come Through The All

Have You Ever Heard A Voice So Powerful That Its Echoes Can Tear Down Brick Walls?

Whoever Says "No Way"

I Just Look Up And Think "Yahweh!"

Change Is Permanent? Or Is That What I Have Just Been Told?

Should We Reign In The New & Throw Out The Old?

God, Only YOU Can Take Back What The Devil Tries To
Control
History, Now That Subject Is Definitely A Mystery
Was It 30 Pieces Of Silver, Or Was It 1000 Pieces Of Gold?
Only YOU Remember What Judas Had Received For Selling
Jesus's Soul?

#6

Bipolar

One Of The Toughest Battles With The Greatest Lesson

Starts With A Curse, But Could End As A Blessing

Lightning Quick & Defying Gravity

Later Exhausted, Detached From Reality

Spiritually Full, But There's A Hollow Cavity

Perfectly Composed

Or Am I Speaking Blasphemy?

#7

¿?

Odin Exchanged An Eye For Wisdom

He Didn't Do It To Become Above The System

Buddha Departed From The Palace To Seek Enlightenment

Don't Think For A Second That Any Of It Was For
Entitlement

Jesus Christ Sacrificed Himself For All Our Wrongs

The Messiah Saved Me, So I Can Type These Poems

"Imagine" & "Let It Be"

What About The Second Martin Luther King?

A Man Who Famously Said "I Have A Dream"

Ronald Reagan Even Spoke Of A Guaranteed Way To Obtain
Peace

Do You Know The Solution To "Houston We Have A
Problem"

I Can't Imagine "Surrender" Being A Word To Solve It

Who Else, What Next, When Shall, & How?

Learn From Our Past, Look To The Future, & Live In The
Now

8 Billion People Can Ask One "Why?"

Not Even I Could Give A Solid Reply

"It's Not Rocket Science, But It's Close Enough To Quantum

Mechanics"

Used To Say It Myself "Don't Panic & Stay Manic"

24

#8

From Prometheus to Zeus

I Know You're Not Big On Forgiveness

And Are More One Of Justice And Vengeance

I Am Sorry, Zeus, For I Did Steal Some Of Your Precious Fire

For My Personal Redemption

I Shared It, Taught It, And At First Claimed It Was Mine

Later On, I Begged For Your Mercy, Now I'm On Your

Borrowed Time

Taking From The Immortal Himself And Giving To The

Mortals In Which Whom You Were Willing To Destroy

Zeus, Forgive Me Later, For You'll Someday Enjoy

I Did Defy, I Did Lie, And Yes, I Tricked

Over Time It Even Made Me, Prometheus, Very Sick, Which

Later It Makes More Sense

Admitted To The Lands From Here And There, Above And

Below, That It Was All Actually YOU

Truth Is A Question, A Lesson, And There's Not An Earthly

Possession That Is True

Were You Wrong, Or Was I Right? Was I Darkness, And You

Were Light?

Oh Zeus, If It Be Anger In Thy Heart, Then Send A Bolt

Down And Strike Me Dead And Cold

Prometheus, For Now, Is Sitting By A Warm Fire Telling The

Tales Of Old

Does Your Name Ever Get Mentioned?

All The Time, But You Never Cared To Listen

30 Pieces Of Silver At 33 Years Of Age?

Christ Chuckles In Love While Judas Plots To Betray

Socrates, Plato, Aristotle, Alexander The Great!

Wisest Man Alive, For I Know Nothing Today

Zeus, I Wasn't Planning On Forever

Cheers, Prost, Toast To Future Endeavors

I Thought I Was Wise

But You, You Were More Clever

#9

"Liar!"

Liar, Liar, Is Your Lair Is On Fire?

No One Can Help You And Your Earthly Desires

The Lord Shall And Will Determine It All

Some Shall Rise, And Many Will Fall

A Psychopath Was Born, And A Sociopath Was Made

But What Is A Blinding Light To An Ever Fading Shade?

Hello Satan, Nice To Meet You, But My Name Is God!

The Lord Can Stand Before You, But You Will Always Run
Off!

Now, Are You Finally Starting To Understand?

Why did Prometheus Stole Fire and Gave It All Back To
Man?

The Lord Truly Knows And The Lord Has Truly Done

For The Lord Is One And All, And Many Of Suns

#10

Dreams

Are Silk Ribbons

Some Gold

Some Blue

Dreams

Are Strange Weavings

Half Broken, Half True

Dreams

Are For Lovers

For Gypsies, For Queens

Dreams

Are Old Sorrows

Life's Patchworks, Its Seams

#11

"Life Is Easy"

Yes Believe Me
To Every Run
The Serious Stress
Is A Wasting One

Just As A Cloud
Upon Light Wind
Life Is Easy
Heat Is Sin

#12

"Tears"

A Tear Trudged Upon The Cheek

Paused, Grew Amazed, Then Floundered To Naught

The Eyes Became Delirious

Forth With Came Tears

#13

Mutual Woe

O Love Forgive
Such Mutual Woe
How Did I Dare
To Smile, And Go?
The Urge I Felt
The Little Care
A Pause To Curse
The Stubborn Air
The Hot Winds Past
I Cherish More
Those Self-Same Words
I Cursed Before!

#14

I Needed You !

When I Could Only Hate
You Taught Me How To Love
When I Was Filled With Doubt
You Showed Me How To Trust
When I Had Known Despair
You Planted Seeds Of Hope
When You Found Me Weeping
Somehow, You Made Me Laugh
When I Had Been Fault-Finding
You Made Me Wise To Praise
When I Had Been Selfish
You Taught Me How To Share
When I Was Darkness
You Led Me To The Light
And I Who Was So Foolish
Am Now Far More Wise
Now That I See The World
Through Someone Else's Eyes
And I Who Was So Blind Can Now More Clearly See
That As You Reached Out To Help
You Must Have Needed Me !

#15

The Teacher

Sighing Winds Are Lonely
They Speak To Me
Of Many Things Past
Remembered Dreams
Loves I Once Knew
The Friends Gone On
They Speak To Me
Of Childhood Things
When Life Was A Shining Ball
And Hopes Were High
When I Had Believed
I Could Conquer All Things
Could Move Mountains
Ford Impossible Streams
Or Reach Great Heights
But That Was Ages Ago
If I Had Just Tried My Wings
And Sadly Learned
I Could Not Fly
Or Reached A River
I Could Not Cross
Or Faced A Mountain

I Could Not Climb

Or Found A Love

That Would Not Stay

Such Things As These

May Have Tried My Soul

Or Left Me Spent

But Oh, What I Learned Along The Way

#16

I Would Go Quietly

I Came Into This World
With No Fanfare
With No Trumpet's Sound
I Live My Life Quietly
I Sought No Limelight
I Loved No Glare
My Life Has Never Been Unseen
I Am Little Known
Save For Those Few
Close To Me Now
So I Would Steal Away
As Quietly As I Came

#17

Things of the Heart

There Is A Tiny Spot
Deep Within My Heart
Where I Have Jealously Guarded
Some Dreams Set Apart
And I Often Go There
To Seek Out These Treasures Old
These Remembrance Of The Past
These Jewels Of Pure Gold
Though Some Have Lost Their Luster
Are Worn And Stained With Tears
They Have Served Me Well
Across The Many Years
So Carefully Have I Guarded Them
That There Was None To See
These Hidden Hopes And Dreams
Those Which Were A Part Of Me
And When This Life Is Over
And The Heart Beats Its Last
I Shall Take Them With Me
These Tokens Of The Past

#18

Light

Through Fields

I Walk

A Silent Scented Path

I Pass In Noonday Heat

I Walk

In The Springtime

Among The Flowers

There

Mingled With The Lotus

I Am Uneven Magic

Untold To A Sleeping World

I Bend With Day

To A Brutal Rest

I End With Eternity

I... Am Light

#19

The Traveler

One Goes To The Left
One Goes To The Right
When The Self-Same
Forces Press
And Who's To Say
Which Went The Right Way
As He Met Life's Strain And Stress
Like A Ship At Sea
Is Each Traveler
As The Journey Onward
He Makes
And 'Tis How He Sets The Sail
And Not The Gale
That Determines The Course
He Takes

#20

Men in Stone

Weep And Moan
Because Hope Drags On
At A Snail's Pace
By Checkered Windows
They Own No Laughter
On Time's Sweet Face

#21

To A Blind Girl

Far Better Blind
Shut From The World
Than To See Or Know
O Little Girl
For Seeing Points
A Dusty Road
And Knowing Is
A Drop Of Blood

#22

Autumn

Once Again, It's October
The World Is Turning Brown
Along The Winding River
That Skirts The Little Town
Beyond The Open Meadows
I See The Mountain High
It Is A Lonely Sentinel
Against A Darkened Sky
Fields Are Dry And Barren
The Fodder Stacked In A Row
While A Field Mouse
Sits Atop The Old Scarecrow
Geese Are Silhouetted
Against The Autumn Sky
They Dip Their Wings To Me
As They Go Hurrying By
And Along A Hedgerow, Where Red Sumacs Abound
A Busy Little Cottontail
Is Burrowing In The Ground

#23

Natural Faith

Faith Is Truly God's Great Gift

Trust In Him

The Clouds Will Lift

Turn To Him In Daily Prayer

Tell Him Every Doubt & Care

Hope In Him When Shadows Fall

His Great Wings Enfold Us All

Even The Sparrow Can Understand

It Is Safe Within His Hands

In The Darkest Of Nights, When Hope Seems Lost

Clinging To My Faith, No Matter The Cost

Through Trials And Tribulations, I Stand Strong

Believing In Something Greater, A Power Beyond

Faith, O' Faith, A Guiding Lighthouse In A Wicked Storm

In The Depths Of My Soul, You Keep Me Warm

I'll Walk Through Fire & Face Every Fear

With Faith As My Shield & Having Nothing But Cheer

In A World Full Of Chaos, Where Doubt Fills The Air

I Hold Onto My Faith Like A Whispered Prayer

A Beacon Of Hope, A Truth Deep Inside

A Strength That Sustains Me In This Turbulent Tide

Through Valleys Of Shadow & Death To

The Mountains Of Paradise & Rest

My Faith Carries Me, It Is A Newfound High

With Each Step I Take, With Every Breath, I Sigh

I'm Filled With A Faith That Will Never Leave

However, Mote It Shall Be

#24

Foreign Directions

New Reflections, Different Perspectives, & Foreign Directions

Am I Breaking Down Or Breaking Through, Like The Dawn
Of Day?

What Do You Want Me To Actually Say?

All I Did Was Meditate & Pray

Dropped The Pieces Of The Puzzle That Didn't Exactly Fit

Never Exactly Noticed The Power Coming From Within

The Wave Tossed In The Ocean & That Vapor In The Wind

I Was Once Known As The 9th Knight Of 99 Sins

Now, There Is An Opportunity To Play Our Hands Again

Came, Saw, & Conquered

The Price Of Paradise Is To Go Completely Bonkers

What Did The Mad Hatter Ask Little Alice?

Why Did Buddha Decide To Leave The Palace?

Wasn't Anakin Supposed To Bring The Balance?

Why Is My Mind Possessed To Even Ask This?

#25

A Goldmine Within My Own Mind

I Sit On A Goldmine Within My Own Mind

Endless Thoughts, Treasures Intertwine

A Wealth Of Ideas Waiting To Shine

Deep In The Abyss, Not Afraid To Explore

Bringing To Light The Darkness That People Adore

Creativity Flows Like Never Before

I Sit On A Goldmine Within My Own Mind

Gold, Like A Treasure Trove

My Imagination Is Always Ready To Roam

Power Of The Mind Is A Force To Behold

Limitless Potential, So I've Been Told

A Goldmine, It's One Of A Kind

Each Creation I Make Leaves The World Behind

A Universe Of Possibilities And Probabilities Are Within My

Scope

A Ray Of Light And A Beacon Of Hope

#26

An Honest Boy

An Honest Boy
Will Build A Bridge
And He Will Cross
To A Sun-Kissed Ridge
He Will Use His Hands
Careless Of Time
With Hammer And Nails
And Shaping Line
And The Doubters
May Scoff At His Bridge
They Will Bless Him The Day
They Too Come To That Ridge

#27

Recovery

In The Depths Of Despair
My Soul Lost In Addiction
Chasing Highs
Drowning In Affliction
A Spiral Of Darkness
A Never-Ending Mission
But In The Midst Of Chaos
A Glimmer Of Hope
A Hand Reaching Out
A Chance To Cope
A Journey Of Healing
A Path To Elope
Through The Pain And The Struggle
A Light Shines Bright
A Heart That's Been Broken
Now Ready To Fight
A Spirit Renewed
Soaring To New Heights
Recovery Is A Journey
Not A Destination
A Daily Commitment
A Transformation

A Life Reclaimed

A Celebration

48

#28

Echoes & Shadows

To My Echo

My Shadow, The One Who Enlightens Me
From The Break Of Dawn To The Retirement Of Nights
You Are Brighter Than The Eastern Star
And Like A Candle, You Cast No Shadow, But Only Light
That Little Flame Will One Day Ignite
A Wildfire So Fierce And Powerful
That Not One Will Want To Fight

#29

Cease-Fire

Truly, Can We Have Thoughts Without Being Considered
Judgmental?
Well, It Can Be Complicated Or Confusing, Yet Possibly
Simple
Throw A Stone In The Pond, And You'll See, Upon Contact,
The Ripples
Cause And Effect, That's Life's Puzzle And Riddle
How Do We Stop All Of Our Desires?
The Question Itself Leads You To Seek Wider And Higher
The Mind Was At War, Now I Declare A Cease-Fire

#30

West Meets East

I Speak To God, And People Say I Am Praying

God Speaks To Me, And The Same Call Me Crazy

In The West, We Use Words Like Broken

Out East, It Could Actually Be Perceived As Chosen

I Do Apologize For Challenging And Questioning The Higher
And Wiser

If We Are Going To Right What Is Left, Then I Could
Probably Use An Advisor

Maybe A Shaman Who Can Understand The Spirits

Then Add In A Doctor Who Is More Scientific And Backed
By Merits

Medication, Meditation, And Them Tough Pills To Swallow

Imagine There Are Some Stranger Things On A Road That
Most Fools Follow

#31

The Door

In Life, You'll Walk Through Many Doors
Some Doors Are Good, Some Bad, Some Confusing
There's This One Special Door Though
You'll Know What I'm Talking About Once You See It
Because It's Different
God Won't Open That Door Until One Is Ready
This Door Has Always Been Right In Front Of Our Faces
It Just One Day Makes More Sense
I Can't Really Explain It, But This Door Is The ONE
Step Into The Frame, Straddle Each Side
Behind You Is The Past, The Framework Is Your Present
Now Take That Step Forward Into The Future
Left Foot, Then Right Foot, And Never Look Back
In One Hand, You Have Love, And In The Other, You Have
Faith
Limitless And Boundless Souls Bringing Love And
Compassion
To A World In Recovery

#32

Peaks & Valleys

An Answer That Is Often Questioned

Curses Worn Openly, But In Nakedness A Blessing

All Poems Eventually Become A Genuine Lesson

And The Love Found Within It

O' A Hidden Treasure

Everything Experienced Will Be Beyond Life's Pleasures

The Peaks & Valleys

Forks In The Road

Winding And Snaking Gravel

Full Of Ecstasy & Sorrow

The Highest Low & The Lowest High

Up & Down, Like The Rise & Fall Of A Tide

#33

The Poet & Sage

I Questioned GOD, And The Lord Proved Me Wrong

Everything Written Is Lyrics To His Song

Who Shall Ever Question The Sword Of The Lord?

The Mystic Sits Down, A Poet Takes The Stage

Poet By Night, Sage Throughout Day

#34

Madman Or Messiah

Rhymes, Riddles, & Deafening Sounds
A Question That Lingers, The Mystery That Bounds
Can I Offer You Clues, Or Will I Lead You Astray?
A Chaotic Challenge That Creates Order From Craze
Am I A Madman, Messiah, Maybe Something More?
A Trickster, A Sage, Or An Open Door?
Perhaps, The All & Nothing, Ceiling & Floor
A Paradox, A Contradiction, Or Someone You Adore
Hopefully, These Words Stir Up Your Mind
Lovely Thoughts That Dance & Whispers That Shine
Asking The Questions That Make You Pause
The Answers That Elude, The Doubts That Solve

#36

Manic

Manic Episodes, Recurring Whirlwinds

A Flurry Of Energy That Cannot Be Tamed

A Rush Of Euphoria, A Feeling Of Grandeur

A Belief That We Are Powerful, A World Of Color

Our Thoughts Race, Our Words Spill Out

A Creative Impulse That Cannot Be Denied

An Energy That Never Seems Shy

We're Invincible, Unstoppable, Unbreakable

A Force To Be Reckoned With, But Is It A Lie?

Yet, As The Storm Rages On, We Begin To Realize

That The Wind That Lifts Us Up Can Also Knock Us Down

The High We Feel Is Fleeting, Temporary

And Soon We're Left To Stare At A Bitter Dawn

Our Loved Ones Watch Helplessly

As We Spiral Out Of Control

They See The Danger, The Risks

But We Are Too Caught Up In The Role

And Then The Crash, The Sudden Descent

As Reality Slams Us Back To The Ground

We See The Wreckage We've Left Behind

And The Guilt And Shame Begin To Surround

But Through It All, We Know One Thing

That This Too Shall Pass, Like All Things Do

And We Will Rise Again, Stronger And Wiser

With A Newfound Compassion For Ourselves And All Who

Knew

For The Human Mind Is Complex And Fragile

And We Navigate Its Twists And Turns As Best We Can

We Are Warriors, Survivors, And Dreamers

And Our Journey Is Nothing Short Of Grand

#37

Fate & Faith

Billions Of Miles, I Can Quickly Drift Away

Yet, I Snap Back Into The Moment When I Begin To Pray

Effectively & Effortlessly, Listen & Communicate

Fate Or Faith? What Is My Pen's Name?

#38

Perception

The Question Of Perception
Is Seeing Truly Believing

Or Do We Tend To See
The Things We Believe?
Is Perception Actually Reality?
What If There Is Something Else Much More Deep?
Everything That We Cannot See

#39

Statement:

The Medium Should Think Himself As A Conduit Between

A Master

Whose Depths He Hasn't Fully Explored

And Potential Students Who Might Exceed His Own Talents

#40

HOLY WATER

7 7 24

Water droplets on the floor

In a pool accepting more

Not knowing where they're from

7 7 24

Underwater thoughts

Not like before

I now wander not alone

7 7 24

The Holy Spirit who came before

Secured my spirit as His own

For this, I am sure.

7 7 24

Water droplets on the floor

Now you know from whence you come

Holy Water from the Son

Diane aka Lucy

#41

The Knight & Jester

There Is A Sacred Place
Where Tales Are Told
The Jester And A Knight
A Story So Old
Jester Employs His Wit
Knight Fights With Might
Both Stand Together Under The Day's Moonlight
A King's Unlikely Duo
Bound By Destiny, But Beyond So True Though
Laughing And Fighting
Side By Side
In A World Where Their Spirits Collide
Quick With The Jokes
One Lightens The Way
Other With His Honor, Never Led Astray
Through Battles And Banquets
They Traveled Far And Wide
Facing Challenges With Courage And Pride
Through The Darkest Of Nights
And The Brightest Of Days
Their Bond Grew Stronger In Many Ways
For The Jester Found Courage

The Knight Found Mirth

In Each Other, They Found Their Own True Worth

All The World Needs Is A Little Love & Hope

They Say If You Love Someone Or Something, Then You'd

Know When To Let Go

#42

Faith

Faith Is Truly God's Great Gift

Trust In Him— The Clouds Will Lift

Turn To Him In Daily Prayer

Tell Him Every Doubt & Care

Hope In Him When Shadows Fall— His Great Wings Enfold

Us All

Even The Sparrow Can Understand, It Is Safe Within His

Hands

In The Darkest Of Nights, When Hope Seems Lost

Clinging To My Faith, No Matter The Cost

Through Trials And Tribulations, I Stand Strong

Believing In Something Greater, A Power Beyond

Faith, O' Faith, A Guiding Lighthouse In A Wicked Storm

In The Depths Of My Soul, You Keep Me Warm

I'll Walk Through Fire & Face Every Fear

With Faith As My Shield & Having Nothing But Cheer

In A World Full Of Chaos, Where Doubt Fills The Air

I Hold Onto My Faith, Like A Whispered Prayer

A Beacon Of Hope, A Truth Deep Inside

A Strength That Sustains Me, In This Turbulent Tide

Through Valleys Of Shadow & Death To The Mountains Of

Paradise & Rest

My Faith Carries Me, It Is A Newfound High
With Each Step I Take, With Every Breath, I Sigh
I'm Filled With A Faith That Will Never Leave
However, Mote It Shall Be

#43

Experience

Once Upon A Time
There Was A Man That Ruled The Stage
Some Would Often Say
"He's A Fool, Yet A Sage"
Wonder If You Could Guess
The Man's Name?
The Joker, Thief, & Simply A King?
A Sorcerer Whose Chords Are Hard To Repeat
Are You Experienced?
Are You Still In A Dream?
Looney Toon, Guru, Etc— It Seems
The Man Was Just Doing His Thing

#44

Praha

The City Of Thousand Spires

History Breathes

The River Winds

Through Ancient Streets

O' Praha, A Diamond In The Rough

With Your Castles And Bridges

You're Gorgeous Enough

Praha, City Of Ten-Hundred Spires

Where The Echoes Of The Past Never Retire

Cobblestone Alleys, Secrets To Inspire

In Your Heart, I Find My Soul's Desire

#45

An Answer That Is Often Question

Curses Worn

In Nakedness

A Blessing

All Poems Eventually Become

A Genuine Lesson

And The Love Found Within It?

O' A Hidden Treasure!

Everything Experienced

Will Be Beyond Life's Pleasures

#46

Breaking News

Reporter: I'm Reporting Alive Here On A Crime Scene
That Leaves A Woman Missing & Presumably Dead
Investigators And Officials Are Stating Witnesses Said
"Someone Screamed Around Midnight & Culprit Fled"
What On The Fuck Is Going On With My Head?
I Have Witnessed Stranger Things, But This One? It Haunts
My Dreams
Traveled Across The Land Of The Living & A Sea Of Screams
Investigators Say, Mrs. Deja Vu Disappeared Mysteriously
Minding My Mind, Simply Riddles & Rhymes, Yet Can The
Rumors True?
Who Is Guilty Of Lying A Time Or Two, And Maybe Few?
How Do We Know If The Innocent Is Telling The Truth?

#47

What If There Exists A Specific Point In Time

What If There Exists A Specific Point In Time
Within Every Journey Of Space
That Requires Woman & Man
A Time Where Both Begin To Understand
What The Two Had Never Known About Yet One That's
Always Been
Virtue & Sin, Yang & Yin, Mr. Beginning & Mrs. End
I Now Pronounce You Wife & Husband

#48

There Stands An Endless Mountain Range

There Stands An Endless Mountain Range That One Must Trek

Flipping The Script & Rewriting The Thousand Wrongs That A Bad Man Left

Often It Had Been Said, The Worst Pain In Life Is A Feeling Of Regret

Call That Place Heaven, Valhalla, Or Maybe To You It Is Shambhala

What If The Orders Came Down And Said, "ABIJAH?"

Who Takes Care Of That Check Of Debt That Is Owed Back To Madam Karma?

The Offer Of Payment Is Insured & Worthy In All Shape & Forms

Once Read This Debate About A Liar, Lunatic, Or Lord

No, God Cannot Be Separate From The Previous Two That Are Mentioned Before

More Like "And" Not To Be Confused With An "OR"

Frozen Solid, But He Can Be Thawed Out Quick With A Flicker Of His Sword That Can Indeed Scorch

Trust Me, I Would Rather Write With And Live A Life For The Lord

It's Just I Already Seen What Happens When One Goes Against The Creator

#49

I Am The Riddle

I Am The Riddle

The Puzzling Enigma

A Question That Lingers

A Mystery To Figure

I Can Offer Clues Or Lead You Astray

A Challenge To Decipher

Night Or Day

Am I A Madman, A Fool

Or Something More

A Trickster, A Sage

Or An Open Door

Perhaps I Am Both

And Yet Neither At All

A Paradox

A Contradiction

Standing In Awe

For I Am The Words That Stir Your Mind

The Thoughts That Dance

The Whispers That Bind

I Am The Questions That Make You Pause

The Answers That Elude

The Doubts That Cause

#50

Hands Pen Over To You

Sharpening The Sword and polishing The Shield,   I march out daily on The Battlefield.   Trusting and Believing that all will be won,   I keep fighting knowing I AM HIS SON"

Pastor Ben Weems

The Rock Church